3099200002990 2

VALENTINE'S DAY

An Easy-Read Holiday Book

VALENTINE'S DAY

by Cass R. Sandak

illustrations by Michael Deas

FRANKLIN WATTS
New York/London/Toronto/Sydney
1980

For U.F.O.

R.L. 2.8 Spache Revised Formula

Library of Congress Cataloging in Publication Data

Sandak, Cass R.
  Valentine's Day.

  (An easy-read holiday book)
  Includes index.
  SUMMARY: Presents the history and customs
of Valentine's Day.
  1. St. Valentine's Day—Juvenile literature.
[1. St. Valentine's Day] I. Deas, Michael. II. Title.
III. Series: Easy-read holiday book.
GT4925.S26   394.2'683   80–10511
ISBN 0-531-04151-4

Valentine's Day is a time when it is nice to tell people we like them. We can do this in a number of ways all through the year. But on Valentine's Day we may send valentines—little cards or notes saying "Be my Valentine."

Grown-ups also like to send valentines. They send each other cards or gifts.

Your father might give your mother a present like flowers or a fancy box of chocolates.

Your mother might give your father a shirt or tie. All of these things say "I love you."

Valentine's Day is not a religious or a legal holiday. It is different from many of our holidays. Schools are open. Stores and banks are open too.

Valentine's Day gets its name from Saint
Valentine. There were a number of saints named
Valentine. The most famous one lived in Rome
around the year 270. At that time, most Romans
still believed in their old gods. Christians could not
worship openly. Many Christians were imprisoned
because their religion was not accepted.

Saint Valentine was a Christian priest who was put in jail for his beliefs. But even in jail he was cheerful and kind. The jailer had a young daughter who was blind. Valentine is said to have cured her blindness. Because of this miracle, he was sentenced to die. On the night before he was to die, Valentine sent a note to the young woman he had cured. He signed the note "From your Valentine." People say that this is why we send valentine messages even today.

Saint Valentine's head was cut off on February 14. At this same time, the Romans were celebrating one of their biggest holidays. Every year on February 15 they celebrated a holiday called the **Lupercalia** (Loo-per-KAY-lee-ah). This was to remember **Lupercus** (Loo-PER-kus), a Roman god who protected the city from wolves.

The day before the Lupercalia was another
Roman holiday. This holiday was for **Juno,** the
queen of the Roman gods. On this day young Roman
men picked the names of girls. These young women
would be their partners in games and dances. This
is why Valentine's Day became a special day for
young people in love.

When the Romans became Christians, the old festival was kept. But old customs were given new meanings. Saint Valentine had died on February 14, and so his name was given to the holiday. And the pairing off of young couples also continued—only now it became part of Valentine's Day.

No one knows exactly when or how Saint Valentine's Day spread from Rome to Northern Europe. For at least five hundred years the holiday has been popular in England. Valentine's Day was first celebrated in America by settlers from the British Isles.

In the Middle Ages young men and women in England, Scotland, and France would pick the names of their valentine sweethearts on the night before Valentine's Day. This was just as the early Romans had done.

Today young people may still put their valentine cards into brightly decorated valentine boxes.

Several interesting ideas about Valentine's Day have come down to us from the past. Many people believe that the first person you see on Valentine's Day will be your valentine. To be awakened by a kiss on Valentine's Day is very good luck. Some people believe that you will see your lover's face in a dream on Valentine's Eve if you sleep with the leaves of certain plants under your pillow.

Birds are often used in valentine pictures. Because birds fly and sing, they seem to stand for freedom and happiness.

Hundreds of years ago, people believed that birds picked their mates on Valentine's Day. Some birds keep the same mates all their lives. This is why they stand for love and faithfulness. We call two people who are very happy together "lovebirds."

In the Middle Ages, and later in the **Renaissance,** young men sent their sweethearts gifts on Valentine's Day. These gifts might be flowers, or birds in a cage. If they were rich, the young men gave very costly gifts. Princes and noblemen would send their ladies gold rings, bracelets, or necklaces.

Sometimes a knight in the Middle Ages wore a token. The token was often a ribbon, a piece of lace, or a handkerchief. This was given to him by his lady love when he rode into battle. Knights wore these tokens to remind them of their love when they fought in **tournaments** (TUR-nah-ments). That is why many valentine cards today are trimmed with ribbons, velvet, satin, or lace. A fancy handkerchief makes a nice valentine gift.

Parties and dances are often held in schools on Valentine's Day. Decorations may have red hearts with arrows through them.

The red heart is a very old sign for love. Years ago, people thought that the heart was the center of our feelings. We still say "I'm broken-hearted" when we are sad. Or we may say "It does my heart good" when we are happy. The heart is also connected with the story of **Cupid,** an ancient Roman god.

The name Cupid comes from the Latin word for desire. The Greeks called this god Eros (E-ross), the god of love. Cupid is usually shown in pictures as a curly-headed, chubby young boy with wings.

In old stories, Cupid flew around shooting arrows into people's hearts. These arrows did not kill them, but made them fall in love with whoever was nearby. Often Cupid shot his arrows with little thought or care. Because of this, the most unlikely people would sometimes fall in love. People say that "Love is blind." This means that many times it is hard to understand why two people fall in love.

People often send flowers as gifts or use them as decorations on Valentine's Day. Since earliest times, roses have been prized as the most beautiful of flowers. Red roses have a special meaning for lovers.

There is an old English saying about the flowers we call "bachelor's buttons." If a man wears them on Valentine's Day he will marry his sweetheart within a year.

The violet is also a Valentine's Day flower. It is said that violets grew outside the window where Saint Valentine was jailed. Some stories say that Valentine spelled out messages with the flowers.

The little cards we call valentines are probably the most popular part of Valentine's Day. People have been sending valentine messages for hundreds of years. There were even books that told how to write valentines.

The first valentine cards in the United States were made by hand about two hundred years ago. People wrote valentine notes or verses on paper. Then they drew designs or pictures around the verses.

About one hundred years ago, companies began to make many kinds of valentines. Some of these were word puzzles. Others had to be folded a certain way to be read.

Some had little mirrors on them to show the faces of the people who got them. Others had photographs of the people who sent them. These were very special valentines. Cameras were new. It took time and money to make a photograph.

Many valentines were decorated with paper lace or designs made with pin holes. Others had pictures or cut-out designs made of cloth. Some of them even had parts that could be moved by pulling little tabs.

Today a large number of valentine cards are sold in stores. You can probably find just the right cards to send to your parents or friends.

Or, better still, you can make your own valentine.

It is easy to make your own valentine from paper and paste and a few other materials. It is best if you have red paper. If you don't, white or any other paper will do.

To make a heart that is even on both sides, fold your paper in half.

Draw half a heart shape along the edge that is folded. Leave the paper folded and cut along the line you have drawn.

You will have a heart that is the same size and shape on each side.

This heart can be decorated with a lace doily, bits of ribbon, leftover wrapping paper, foil, or any other things you might have around the house. You can draw a picture to put in the middle of the heart. Or you can cut figures out of cloth or paper. You can paste pictures cut from a magazine on your valentine.

You can make your valentine just as fancy as you like. You could even glue pieces of uncooked macaroni onto your valentine heart. Use your imagination!

When the valentine is finished you can write a message on it. Then send it to someone you like— your parents or a special friend. If you like somebody but want to keep it a secret, it is all right to send a valentine signed "Guess who?"

It is fun to know why we celebrate Valentine's Day the way we do. Every time we follow an old custom we give new meaning to the holiday. Valentine's Day customs have a long history. But every time we send a valentine, the message is new. We say "I like you" or "I love you."

INDEX

DATE DUE

AP 14'81 FEB 21 1992 108 T-106			
FE 12'82 T.114			
FE 19'82 FEB 105 103			
JAN 20 1984 OCT 18 104			
JAN 25 FEB 5			
110 FEB 12			
FEB T113			
FEB 15 1984			
FE 11 110			
FEB 15 105			
FEB 14 105			
FEB 19 1987 113,106			
JAN 28 1988			
FEB 11 1988			
FEB 9 101 1990 106			
114			
FEB 24 1991			
FEB 21 1991 104			